COPYRIGHT 2018, 2017 by Pinecrest Street Company

All rights reserved. This publication is protected by Copyright laws. No part of this book may be reproduced, stored in a retrieval system, or transmitted in any form, or by any means electronic, mechanical, photocopying, recording, or otherwise with prior permission of Pinecrest Street Company, and as expressly permitted by the applicable copyright status. Dissemination or sale of any part of this book is not permitted. Request for written permission may be obtained by writing Pinecrest Street Company, LLC. 11301 S. Dixie Hwy. Box 5666684, Miami FL 33256. Pinecrest Street Company crest is a trademark of Pinecrest Street Company, Inc. and is registered in the United States.
ISBN 978-1-7323690-0-9

Executive Editor: Carlos Borges
Authors: Kay Lopate and Patsy Self Trand
Book Design and Layout: Ana Garcia and Alexa Behm
Published independently by Pinecrest Street Company, LLC.
www.pinecreststreetcompany.com
Address 11301 S. Dixie Hwy. Box 566684 Miami FL 33156
Printed in the United States

Taking on the Challenge Series

Making it to GRADUATION

EXPERT ADVICE FROM COLLEGE PROFESSORS
RESEARCHED AND WRITTEN BY

KAY LOPATE, PH. D.   **PATSY SELF TRAND, PH. D.**

Books Published by Pinecrest Street Company, Inc.

College Bound Series: Knowing What to Expect – Preparing for "A's"

30 Awesome reading and learning strategies for high school students. (2017). Trand, Patsy Self and Lopate, Kay. Pinecrest Street Company.

Become a great college reader: Get the basics of reading now before you begin college. Book 1. (2017). Lopate, Kay and Trand, Patsy Self. Pinecrest Street Company.

Getting the basics of critical thinking for college readers and writers. Book 2. (2018). Lopate, Kay and Trand, Patsy Self. Pinecrest Street Company.

Challenge Series: Success in Difficult Courses – Making "A's"

Making it to Graduation: Expert advice from college professors (2nd, ed.) (2018). Lopate, Kay and Trand, Patsy Self. Pinecrest Street Company.

The Official Parent Playbook: Getting your child through college. (2nd, ed.) (2018) Lopate, Kay and Trand, Patsy Self. Pinecrest Street Company.

Making it in Medical School: Expert advice from college professors. (2019). Lopate, Kay and Trand, Patsy Self. Pinecrest Street Company.

Making it in Nursing School: Expert advice from college professors. (2019). Trand, Patsy Self, and Lopate, Kay. Pinecrest Street Company.

The athletes' playbook for college success. (2018). Trand, Patsy Self and Lopate, Kay. Pinecrest Street Company.

"Vocabulary university professors say that every college student should know. (2017). Trand, Patsy Self and Lopate, Kay. Pinecrest Street Company.

Navigating Through College and Beyond Series – Making more "A's"

Capturing the Experience: My child's first year in college. (2nd,ed.) (2017) Lopate, Kay and Trand, Patsy Self, Carpenter, Sara, Pinecrest Street Company.

Capturing the Experience: My first year in college. (2nd,ed.) (2017) Lopate, Kay and Trand, Patsy Self, Carpenter, Sara, Pinecrest Street Company.

Reading and Learning the Required College Courses in the Historical and Social Sciences. Book 3. (2017). Trand, Patsy Self and Lopate, Kay. Pinecrest Street Company.

Reading and Learning the Required College Courses in the Biological and Mathematical Sciences. Book 4 (2017). Trand, Patsy Self and Lopate, Kay. Pinecrest Street Company.

30 Amazing reading and learning strategies for college students. (2017). Lopate, Kay and Trand, Patsy Self. Pinecrest Street Company.

Why I didn't come to class. (2018). Trand, Patsy Self and Lopate, Kay. Pinecrest Street Company.

PINECREST STREET COMPANY, LLC.
Pinecrest Street Publishing
www.pinecreststreetcompany.com
Pinecrest Street Company, LLC
11301 S. Dixie Hwy. POBox 566684
Pinecrest, FL 33256

ABOUT ME

NAME:

HIGH SCHOOL:

COLLEGES APPLIED TO:

COLLEGES I WILL ATTEND:

INTENDED MAJORS:

MY CAREER GOALS:

Table of Contents

- **1** Introduction
- **3** Write a Letter to Yourself
- **6** Before School Begins
- **9** 25 Essential College Supplies
- **10** Time Management
- **12** Improving Your Memory
- **16** Keeping Track of Your Money
- **18** Get-Aways and Holidays
- **20** Top 10 Best Inexpensive Getaways
- **23** Protecting What You Value Most
- **26** Professors Are People Too
- **30** Keeping Up With Classes

33	Confucius says
36	Reading Textbooks
40	People Who Read Books
42	Lecture Classes and Notes
46	Staying Healthy
48	Studying and Preparing for Tests
50	15 Ways to Save in College
54	Being Happy Socially
58	Staying Emotionally and Physically Sound
62	Planning Ahead
66	Staying on Track to Graduate
70	Vocabulary
77	Final Thoughts

WELCOME TO COLLEGE!

Many people say these next four years are the most exciting time in your life. Beginning college is like getting a new start on life. And, you are the one responsible for your success.

This book has a lot of sound advice to help you become the student you want to be intellectually, socially, and academically.

The information in this book is the "unwritten course" that is never taught but you are expected to know!

On the next page, write a letter to yourself.

Notice that each paragraph begins with a sentence starter. All you need to do is add 2-3 sentences to complete the paragraph.

This letter that you write at the beginning of college will help preserve many wonderful memories. When you complete college, during graduation week, we are asking you to complete another letter (in the appendix). We predict that you will be surprised to realize the impact that college had on your life.

A few years from now we would like you to complete the letter on page 79. This is the letter you will write during graduation week. As you recall your years in college, you will be glad you took the time to write all about your experiences and accomplishments.

Date: _____

Dear: _____

Being a college student is an extraordinary opportunity to:
_____
_____
_____

I want to major in: _____
And become a: _____
Because: _____
_____

I know there's no place like home, but: _____
_____
_____

During college I want to become involved in: _____
_____
_____

Some of the things I am concerned about in college are:
_____
_____
_____

I know I will miss _____
I'm very excited about _____
_____
_____

Regards to myself,

THE ONLY PERSON YOU ARE DESTINED TO BE IS THE PERSON YOU DECIDE TO BE.

RALPH WALDO EMERSON

BEFORE SCHOOL BEGINS

OFF TO A GOOD START!

DON'T RUSH into a major. Most students switch majors at least once.

BUY books early and spend an hour browsing through each one.

REGISTER for classes as soon as you can. Some classes fill quickly and close. You don't want to spend an extra year because you could not get in a class.

THINK carefully before taking an 8:00 a.m. class.

MAKE SURE your cell phone will work on campus.

BUY A PLANNER and separate notebook for each class. After you get a syllabus from each class, transfer all your due dates and test dates on the planner. It's OK to use your cell phone as a planner; but, we think a monthly planner (the kind you write in) is more efficient. If you use your phone, set the alarm to give yourself a one week advance warning that something is due.

KNOW how to contact the campus police in case of an emergency.

BUY a whiteboard and a set of colored markers.

GREEK LIFE

Consider the pros and cons of Greek life. Don't commit until you know exactly how this may affect your college experience. Ask yourself if the people in the fraternity or sorority are the kind of people you want to socialize with for the next four years.

RADIATE KINDNESS

Characteristics such as generosity, politeness, honestly, integrity, confidence, empathy, and respect do not happen by chance; they must be cultivated and developed! These values are appreciated and sought after in academic settings as well as in the workplace.

READ THE SYLABUS

As soon as you receive all your syllabi, read each one several times. A syllabus is the contract that has all the rules and assignments. Make sure you transfer important "due dates" to your monthly planner or phone.

AIM HIGH

Set some expectations for yourself. Now is the time to aim high—to do more than you ever thought possible! If you want to, you can even completely remake yourself.

KEEP IN TOUCH

Write down important family and friends' addresses, birthdays, phone numbers and other important dates.

TIME TO ADJUST

Expect that adjusting to dorm life may take three months.

MAJOR LEAGUE

High school was like the minor leagues. Now you are entering college. Think of it as the major leagues.

A BAD BEGINNING MAKES A BAD ENDING

EURIPIDES

I WISH I HAD IT

The 25 Essential College Supplies

- [ ] Cell phone
- [ ] Extension cords
- [ ] Laptop
- [ ] Drivers's license or state I.D.
- [ ] Food bars and snacks
- [ ] Scissors/stapler
- [ ] Common sense
- [ ] Backpack
- [ ] Shower caddy
- [ ] Batteries
- [ ] Flash drives
- [ ] Calculator
- [ ] Flip flops
- [ ] Tissues
- [ ] Flashlight
- [ ] Sewing kit
- [ ] Bathing suit
- [ ] First Aid Kit
- [ ] Hand vacuum
- [ ] Phone charger
- [ ] External power pack
- [ ] Rain gear
- [ ] Earphones
- [ ] Water bottle
- [ ] Aspirin

TIME MANAGEMENT

Save time by listening to recorded lectures with the device set at **TWICE** the playback speed.

ALWAYS be on time or, better still, be a little early. Never be late for classes, meetings, and other appointments. Usually important announcements and assignments are made at the beginning of classes and meetings.

Treat college like an 8-hour day, 40-hour a week **JOB**.

Unplug social media and mobile devices for **TWELVE HOURS** a day.

10% of your time will be in class; **90%** of your time will not be in class!!

Instead of having "back to back classes", schedule time before class to **PREPARE** and after class to review. Serious students like to schedule a free hour between classes so they can **REVIEW** the class they just had and preview the next class. This is an amazing way to "cut down" the amount of study time you would normally have to do during the evening.

It is common for a new college freshman to think there is "nothing to do" or "there is so much time before my next test". Keep reminding yourself that there is **ALWAYS** something you can do for your classes.

Now that you're in college there's **NO ONE** to remind you to get things done.

DON'T overcommit.

Procrastinators always say, "I'll do it tomorrow." The biggest problem with procrastinating is that you'll have less time to study and it may lead to **ANXIETY ISSUES.**

GET UP when the alarm goes off. Better still; put the alarm on the other side of the room. You may want to choose another cell ringtone to make waking up easier.

Go to the library between classes and remember to **LOG OUT** of library computers.

Make some time for **YOURSELF** every day.

Keep an **OPEN** mind.

Take ten minutes at least five times a week and make a **"TO-DO"** list to schedule your assignments and appointments. Although you may think using ten minutes is a waste of time, those ten minutes will probably save you hours later on.

Don't judge too **QUICKLY.**

Do most of your work (studying) during the week so you can have more time for **WEEKEND FUN.**

Be aware of **TIMEWASTERS**: a cluttered desk, not being able to say no, video games, TV, and drop-in visitors.

The amount of material learned is directly related to the amount of **TIME SPENT** on the task.

When someone says they'll only be a minute, they usually take **LONGER.**

Wear a **WATCH** in addition to relying on your phone to tell time.

Lots of successful students study a few hours on a **FRIDAY NIGHT** before they go out and socialize.

Keeping up with your studies is easier than **CATCHING UP.**

Learn to say **"NO".**

IMPROVING YOUR *Memory*

NO ONE IS BORN WITH WITH A GREAT MEMORY

1 Keep a stack of Post-Its in your room and use them to write the material you intend to remember. Stick these Post-Its all over your room. By doing this, you will look at it at least 8-9 times during the day.

2 Review your notes immediately after class or at least the same day. Don't let 48 hours go by without reviewing the material. If too much time goes by without a review, in all likelihood, you will have forgotten most of the material.

3 People become better at skills they practice. Find time to practice the skills you need. For example, you may need to practice your math problems over and over. Keep reminding yourself that a high level of proficiency in anything (sports, music, or academics) requires practice.

4 If something is really important and you need to remember it well, use your three basic modalities: **Visual** (learning from a drawing, picture, chart, or reading); **Auditory** (learning by reading aloud or listening), and **Kinesthetic** (learning by making physical movements relating to the material or by writing summaries, making up questions, or outlining).

5 Make digital flashcards.

6 Remind yourself to think about the material even when you are not in class or studying at your desk. As you walk to class, exercise, drive, or wait for something, recall the information you just learned. This will help get the information into your long-term memory and will be readily accessible when you need it for a test.

7 You can still become rich with an average I.Q.

8 You will remember more if you review a lot. When you review, you are taking the information out of your short-term and transferring it to your long-term memory. If you have reviewed something at least five times, you have created a well-defined link or path from where it was stored in the brain to the place where you need the information. Keep in mind that people vary in the number of times it takes to memorize or remember something.

9 Writing things down is the best secret of a good memory.

TOO MANY PEOPLE SPEND MONEY THEY EARNED TO BUY THINGS THEY DON'T WANT AND TO IMPRESS PEOPLE THEY DON'T LIKE.

— RALPH WALDO EMERSON

KEEPING TRACK OF YOUR money

You will **probably** be broke MOST of the time

Today almost **half** of the college students are in DEBT

Although you are enrolled in college, you can still KEEP searching and applying for **scholarships.**

BEWARE of credit card scams. Remember that if you don't pay your credit card bill on time, a ten dollar item may end up costing fifty dollars! Be skeptical when a credit card offer seems **too good to be true.**

If you **cannot** control spending CUT UP your credit card.

Know **all the facts** before taking out a student loan.

For every dollar borrowed expect to pay back about $3.00

Get a **bank account** in town and get a credit or debit card.

Show appreciation to your parents for paying all or part of your college EXPENSES

DON'T hang out with BIG SPENDERS

Protect your credit and your identity. Make a copy of the contents in your wallet: student ID, passport, credit cards, insurance cards, and other important documents. Store the information in your phone as well as sending a copy or an email to your parents and to yourself.

A bicycle can save you **a lot of time** and you won't get parking tickets.

Buy your snacks at the **local grocery store** rather than at the campus store.

MAYBE!

The real measure of your wealth is how much you'd be worth if you **lost all your money.**

Avoid "SPLURGE" spending.

getaways & holidays

Many students can't wait to go home for Thanksgiving and Christmas break and then are surprised to discover they can hardly wait to get back to school.

book it!

Make your airline reservations at least three months before your break or vacation begins.
Be sure to check all syllabi to make sure you aren't leaving before test dates and other class obligations.

study abroad!

Every college and university has a travel abroad program.
Many ask students to participate in fundraising to earn a considerable amount of their expense of traveling abroad.
The fundraising is usually done one year prior to traveling.

*Some colleges o er alternative breaks such as college courses or volunteering in the U.S. and abroad.

take lots of pictures!

go camping!

For budget conscious students, consider a camping trip to a state or national park. Investigate Airbnb, couchsurfing, hostels, and Craigslist for inexpensive accommodations.

spend wisely!

Avoid (as much as possible) going into debt over a vacation.
Don't make the mistake of using student loans for a wild spring break trip.

TOP 10 BEST INEXPENSIVE GETAWAYS

1. Inexpensive cruise
2. Nearby beaches and lakes
3. Go to a city or town of interest or an unknown destination and spend the day seeing the attractions in that area
4. Hiking
5. "Sleepcation"
6. Week of Intensive Exercise
7. Camping
8. Rent an ATV at state park and ride on the trails—bring a bag lunch and cold water
9. Community theaters and shows
10. Local museums, opera, ballet, and other cultural events

TIP 1:

USE TRIP ADVISOR OR LONELY PLANET FOR ATTRACTIONS AND RECOMMENDATIONS.

TIP 2:

CHECK GROUPON AND SIMILAR SITES FOR "GOOD DEALS."

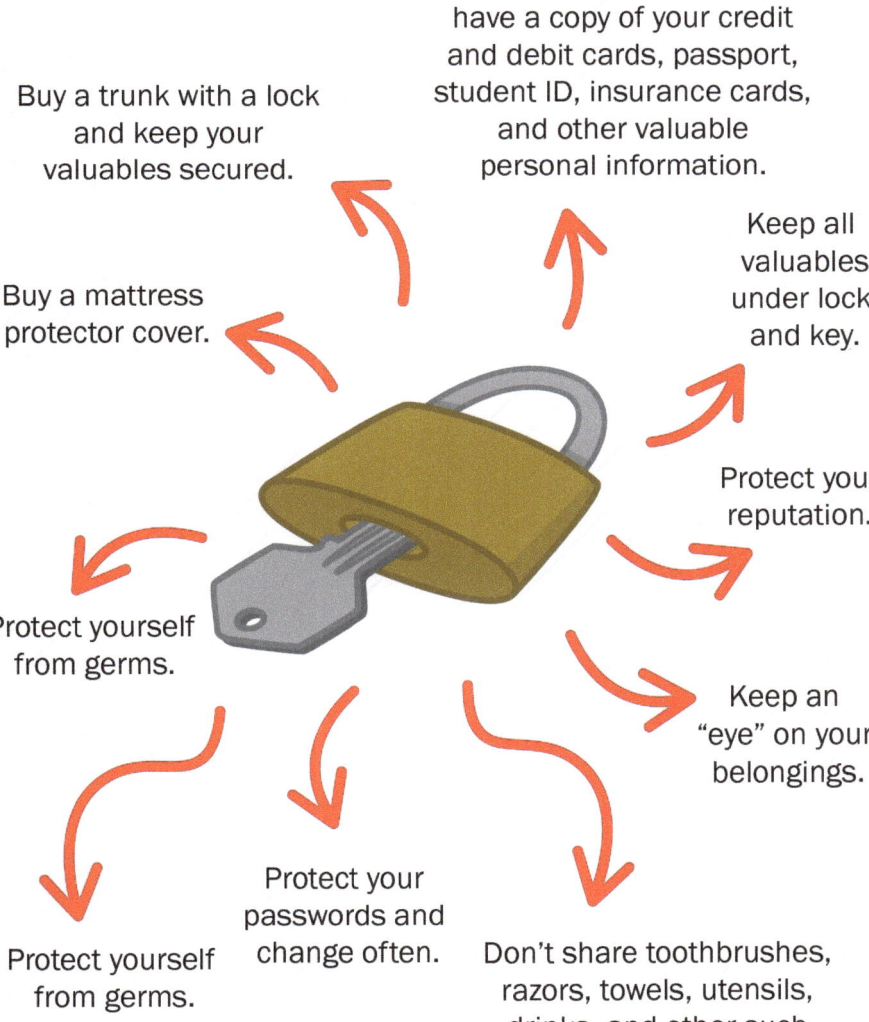

YOUR PROFESSORS
ARE PEOPLE TOO!

DON'T BE SURPRISED
if your professor has a foreign accent that is difficult to understand.

TEACHING IS ONLY PART
of your professor's job. In most cases, research and publishing are their priorities.

STUDENTS MAY NOT
realize this, but professors can see almost everything going on from their position at the front of the room.

COLLEGE PROFESSORS
rarely give extra credit. But, if they do, take advantage of that opportunity.

READ FACULTY EVALUATIONS
when you choose classes but be aware that some professors are only popular because they are easy graders and have engaging personalities.

SOME PROFESSORS ONLY GIVE ONE OR TWO A'S IN THEIR COURSES

NOT ALL PROFESSORS ARE GOING TO REMIND YOU OF A DUE DATE

PROFESSORS KNOW

from experience that most of the "goof-offs" or "slackers" sit in the last few rows.

IF YOU HAVE A TENDENCY

to be shy with professors, keep reminding yourself that they like talking to students.

LEARN TO DEAL

Try not to be shy with professors, keep reminding yourself that they like talking to students.

THERE IS A HIERARCHY

of faculty. The top group are referred to as full or associate professors, the middle group as the assistant professors or instructors, and the lower group are lecturers and adjunct faculty. At many universities doctoral students teach classes as part of their program.

VISIT DURING OFFICE HOURS. PROFESSORS ARE PROBABLY THE MOST UNDERUSED RESOURCE.

YOUR PROFESSORS
THE DO'S AND DON'TS

DON'T Complain to the dean or department chairperson about a professor.

DO Instead of having "back to back classes," schedule time before class to prepare and after class to review. Serious students like to schedule a free hour between classes so they can review the class they just had and preview the next class. This is an amazing way to "cut down" the amount of study time you would normally have to do during the evening.

DO If you know beforehand that you will be missing class, let your professor know. Some instructors adhere to an attendance policy and you could fail by missing more than three classes.

DON'T If you were absent, never say this to a professor, "Did we do anything important in the class I missed?" Never say, "I was absent when you assigned this."

DON'T show up at the professor's office just to complain about a grade. Avoid being defensive.

DON'T Make lame excuses or lie to professors. They have heard them all.

DON'T Be surprised if your professor does not respond to emails or text messages.

DON'T Begin a conversation with a professor by saying, "I've tried to find you many times but you are never there."

DO Something to let your professor know you are not a slacker.

DON'T Expect your college professors to make exceptions just for you.

DO Keep in touch with your favorite professors.

DON'T Be surprised if your professor has a foreign accent that is difficult to understand.

DON'T Blame your professors, your roommate, or your friends for your failures.

> **I WENT TO CLASS BECAUSE I DID NOT HAVE ANYWHERE ELSE TO GO AND IT WAS A FABULOUS HANG.**
>
> **TO MY SURPRISE, WHILE I WAS THERE I LEARNED SOMETHING.**
>
> — RAMSEY SELF

KEEPING UP
WITH YOUR CLASSES

College classes don't meet every day. They usually meet two or three times a week although some classes only meet once a week. Expect a lot of information to be learned in a short amount of time. The amount of material for a semester college course will be the same amount that a high school course has in one year. This means that in college you are expected to learn a lot independently.

Do homework even if it is optional.

In high school you usually have to just memorize facts; in college professors assume you know the facts. Their questions require you to use the facts for inferential thinking and conceptualizing.

Turn off all your technology while in class except a laptop.

Keep a notepad and pencil on your nightstand. Great ideas can come during the night.

Go to every class. You'll have regrets when you start failing.

Good grades don't automatically appear just because you went to every class and did all the assigned work.

At least once a week, "speak up" in class. Before the class you might prepare a few questions from the lecture material or textbook. Change your scenery by having two or three different places to study. Don't use caffeine after 4:00pm because caffeine will disrupt sleep.

At large schools, you may be put on a waiting list to get into the course you want. This can delay your graduation date.

The kind of writing needed for college essays and papers is different than the kind of writing for text messaging.

Don't get addicted to Netflix.

Basically there are three types of college students in every class: The surface learners (they do as little as possible and are satisfied if they pass); the attention seekers (they work for high grades abut are more interested in grades and GPA than in deep understanding); the deep learners (they acquire knowledge and a rich understanding which they connect to the outside world).

Go to the library between classes. Many students report that they can get more done during 20 minutes in the library then two hours in their room or residence hall. Just remember to avoid the social section of the library and find a quiet place.

Have a separate notebook for each class.

Try to sit near the front of the class because it helps keep you focused, improves listening, and helps the instructor get to know you better.

Doing homework is not the same as studying.

Successful students persist and keep going when "the going gets rough". Less successful students give up easily. They quit when they get frustrated or when they do less well than others.

Try to include more active learning techniques. Some active learning techniques are putting the material in your own words, creating diagrams and charts, predicting questions for an upcoming exam, summarizing, and teaching the information to someone else. Passive learning activities are reading, copying notes, looking over notes, or rereading the notes.

Avoiding math classes will prevent you from pursuing medical school, law school, or a Master's Degree in Business. Most colleges and universities offer free math tutoring.

Keep returned papers, quizzes, and other sources of instructor feedback for later review.

Your instructor is there to teach, not to entertain you. Get used to the fact that most of the time your classes will not be fun and exciting---a college degree is the result of commitment and hard work.

Think twice before you skip a class. Based on a 15 week semester for a class that meets three times a week, here is what each class costs (based on tuition).

DARTMOUTH COLLEGE
(Private) $138 a class

UNIVERSITY OF TEXAS
Instate Resident $27.25 a class
Out of State $97 a class

SCOTTSDALE COMMUNITY COLLEGE
Instate Resident $7.08 a class
Out of State $27.17 a class

UNIVERSITY OF WASHINGTON
Instate Resident $32.89 a class
Out of State $94.84 a class

When tempted to skip learning opportunities, consider: **"There are no uninteresting subjects; there are only uninterested people."-Gilbert K. Chesterton**

Take a speech class even if you don't want to. Remember the value of good communication.

Save time by going to the library when it's practically empty and go to the dining hall early.

Often good students request tutoring because this gives them the opportunity to discuss topics with someone who knows the subject very well.

Even though some introductory freshman classes have over 200 students, get to know someone in each class because there will be times when you will have to help each other.

"Reserve Readings" are the books, articles, photographs, and other material that the professor has placed in the library and which cannot be checked out. If it is required reading, make sure you don't wait until the end of the semester.

Learning Centers provide help in study skills, arrange for tutoring and make accommodations for students diagnosed with learning difficulties.

The top two reasons why students fail out or leave school are not keeping up with homework and study and not going to class.

Turn in all assignments. Getting a low score on a paper or assignment is better than receiving a zero. Don't eat, drink, snap gum, unwrap food, or click your pen unnecessarily during class.

Introduce yourself to the person sitting next to you in class.

Being willing to ask for help is the most important resource a student has.

Depending on the class, your final grade may be determined by only a few factors.

Try not to leave class until you feel confident you understand what was presented in that class. If you need further clarification, get help as soon as possible.

One in three college freshmen do not make it to the sophomore year. Some of the reasons are loneliness, family issues, financial problems, and academic struggles.

If your goal is to make A's, remember this: It's not how smart you are, it's the amount of time you are willing to devote to learning.

You need to know the first semester is usually the most difficult.

Once a week ask yourself, "Am I ready to be tested on all the material thus far?"

CONFUCIUS SAYS

> Choose a job you love, and you will **never have to work** a day in your life.

> Life is **really simple**, but we insist on making it complicated.

> The **superior man** is modest in his speech but exceeds in his actions.

> When it is obvious that the goals cannot be reached, don't adjust the goals-- **adjust the action steps.**

> The man who asks a question is a fool for a minute, the man who does not ask is **a fool for life.**

ANY FOOL CAN KNOW.

THE POINT IS TO *understand.*

ALBERT EINSTEIN

READING *textbooks*

YOU BOUGHT THEM, NOW BE SURE TO USE THEM!

A college education is based on reading. At school we first learn to read and then we read to learn. Here are some reading tips to get you going.

Keep a thesaurus and a dictionary at your desk or know how to access these on your cell phone.

Write in your textbook. Don't cheat yourself by keeping it in mint condition so you can sell it back.

Reference librarians are a great source.

They can lead you to the most amazing references.

When highlighting, use a different color for each class.

Develop an interest in the world. It's important to keep up with national and international news. Spend a half an hour each day reading a respected newspaper.

The key to good comprehension is background knowledge.
If you already know something about a topic, you will be able to understand the new information better than someone who knew absolutely nothing about the topic. For example, in an art history class, you will understand a lot about Claude Monet's impressionistic paintings if you had visited his home and gardens in Giverny, France.

BUY THE GUIDE.
Find out if the publisher of your textbook has supplemental teaching aids such as a study guide. Consider buying this because it is a great tool for reviewing.

ENJOY IT!
Read for pleasure because it will expose you to good writing which will help in your own writing.

Reading is important but understanding is even more important.
Don't be the type of reader who keeps reading and after a few pages he/she realizes nothing was understood.

Don't Be Concerned
if you are a slow reader because reading speed is overrated.
Be Concerned
about whether or not you are learning and comprehending.

READ THE SYLLABUS!
You will have a syllabus for every class. Make a copy for your notebook, one for your study area, and one to store in your phone. A syllabus is a contract or rules of the course as set by the professor. Read your syllabus several times. The syllabus will let you know beforehand what you need to do to get a good grade.

DO NOT BUY UNDERLINED OR HIGHLIGHTED BOOKS.
(You have no idea whether the former owner earned an A or an F.)

According to the National Assessment of Educational Progress (April 27, 2016), commonly referred to as the nation's report card, only 1/3 of 12th graders were ready for college level courses.

The percentage of 12th graders who were proficient in reading were:

White 46%
Black 17%
Hispanic 25%
Asian 49%
Island Pacific/American Native 28%
Two or more races 45%
Male 33%
Female 42%

Does Your Mind Wander?

If you find your mind wanders while reading, try this technique:

1. Open your textbook to a reading assignment.

2. Set your watch and read for five minutes.

3. Then take out a sheet of paper and write as much as you can remember from the five minute reading.

4. If you are unable to remember very much, re-read the section.

This is a great monitoring technique and before long you will find you are doing less and less mindless reading.

Always memorize the bold vocabulary words in your textbook.

Two questions to ask after reading a paragraph or a section are:

- **WHAT'S THE POINT?**
- **WHAT SHOULD I LEARN FROM THIS?**

Try to put the information in your own words. This will help to remember it.

When reading material is difficult, try treading out loud or reading into a recorder and listening.

PEOPLE WHO READ BOOKS

- HAVE LARGER VOCABULARIES
- ARE SMARTER
- HAVE A CURRENT VIEW OF THE WORLD
- HAVE MORE IMAGINATION
- HAVE BETTER WRTING SKILLS
- ARE MORE INTERESTING

READING GOAL
READ 12 BOOKS A YEAR!

AN **INVESTMENT** IN KNOWLEDGE PAYS THE BEST INTEREST.

RALPH WALDO EMERSON

LECTURE CLASSES

BLEND IN OR STAND OUT

Always come to class prepared with your textbook, syllabus, a notebook with past class notes, handouts, paper, and pens.

When taking notes, pretend they are for someone else.

Not all professors have review sessions!

Always date and number your lecture notes.

Sit in the front. Those who sit in the back are usually not known to the professor.

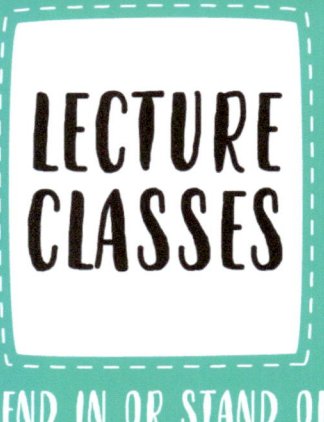

A lot of lecture information will not be found in your textbook. Furthermore, a lot of your education will be learned outside of class.

Learn how to stay awake in class.

Some students think that all they have to do is show up at a lecture class. Although that's important, you can accelerate your learning by incorporating the 3 stages of learning information from lecture presentations.

There are some things you can do before, during, and after the lecture:

THE BEFORE STAGE

Before the lecture you can prepare by looking at the syllabus and knowing what will be the topic of the lecture, take 5-15 minutes to preview (glide through) the corresponding textbook pages, and take note of the vocabulary, terms, names, and events. Pay attention to the drawings, photographs, charts, graphs, and other visual displays and try to understand what is their purpose or what are you supposed to learn from them.

THE DURING STAGE

is the actual time you are in lecture class. In this stage you will take many notes. The quality of your notes will depend on how well you prepared for The lecture or the amount of background knowledge you already have about the topic.

THE AFTER STAGE

is the editing stage. After the lecture, you will read through your notes, fill in gaps, identify topics emphasized in the lecture, and predict a few questions that a professor might ask on a test. The editing stage should be completed within 24 hours after the lecture

YOU ARE THE AUTHOR OF YOUR LECTURE NOTEBOOK!

A HEALTHY ATTITUDE IS CONTAGIOUS BUT DO NOT WAIT TO CATCH IT FROM OTHERS. *Be a carrier!*

THOMAS STOPPARD

25 WAYS TO STAY HEALTHY

Mom won't be there to take care of you!

- **TAKE** A DAILY **SHOWER**
- **EAT** BREAKFAST EVERY DAY
- **DON'T SHARE**
- **MAINTAIN** DENTAL **HYGIENE**
- **USE** SUNSCREEN
- **WASH** YOUR HANDS **FREQUENTLY**
- **TAKE THE STAIRS** AND WALK THE LONG ROUTE **TO CLASS**
- **LEARN** PROPER **PORTION** CONTROL
- **KEEP A POSITIVE** ATTITUDE
- **EXERCISE DAILY**
- **DON'T SMOKE**
- **SLEEP** 7-8 HOURS **EVERY NIGHT**
- **STAY HYDRATED**

TAKE YOUR VITAMINS

EAT 5 servings of **FRUITS** AND **VEGETABLES** every day.

DON'T fight stress **BY EATING**

MAKE SURE you have your **VACCINATIONS**

KEEP ROUTINE DOCTORS VISITS

BRING lunch instead **OF BUYING LUNCH**

KEEP HEALTHY SNACKS around.

DON'T EAT PROCESSED FOOD

DON'T allow others to influence you TO DO ANYTHING

ALWAYS USE GOOD JUDGEMENT & MAKE GOOD DECISIONS

STAY AWAY FROM NARCOTICS AND OTHER SYNTHETIC DRUGS

LIMIT caffeine AND SUGAR

STUDYING & PREPARING FOR TESTS

There are fewer tests in college than in high school but they count more toward the overall grade.

HOW WELL YOU PERFORM ON A TEST IS ALL ABOUT PREPARATION. IF YOU ARE VERY WELL PREPARED, YOU WILL DO WELL.

Start preparing for exams the first day of classes.

Begin studying at least three days before a test.

CREATE ARTIFICIAL DEADLINES.

Don't pin your hopes on the final.

SOMETIMES THE HARDEST PART OF STUDYING IS GETTING STARTED.

Try to actually learn in class rather than telling yourself you'll learn it later.

Avoid marathon study sessions. Study in blocks of one hour and take a five minute break after each.

RELEARNING CAN BE A REAL TIME WASTER.

DO MATH PROBLEMS OVER AND OVER AGAIN.

ONCE A WEEK LOOK AT YOUR NOTES AND TRY TO PREDICT A FEW QUESTIONS THAT YOU THINK THE INSTRUCTOR MIGHT ASK ON A QUIZ.

It's possible to "blank out" on a test but don't expect your professor to be forgiving about the grade

Try to learn the material the first time it is presented.

Study at least a week before a major exam so you don't have to rely on an "all-nighter" and Red Bull.

Do homework even if you know it will not be collected.

DON'T WAIT FOR AN EXAM TO STUDY.

Have no more than three people in a study group. Otherwise it might become a party.

USE NOISE CANCELING HEADPHONES IF YOU ARE EASILY DISTRACTED.

EVERYTHING PRESENTED IN CLASS IS FAIR GAME FOR THE TEST!

Professors use different types of tests. Students report that the easiest tests are multiple choice and true/false. More difficult tests are fill in the blank, sentence completion, and matching. The most difficult tests for many are the essay tests.

Prepare for each class as though there would be a pop quiz.

For an upcoming test, use your syllabus as an outline for a study guide.

FIND AT LEAST ONE DEPENDABLE PERSON IN EVERY CLASS IN CASE YOU NEED TO CLARIFY SOMETHING. MAKING PRACTICE TESTS IS ONE OF THE BEST LEARNING TECHNIQUES.

WE LEARN

10% OF WHAT WE READ;
20% OF WHAT WE HEAR;
30% OF WHAT WE SEE;
50% OF WHAT WE SEE AND HEAR;
70% OF WHAT WE DISCUSS;
80% OF WHAT WE EXPERIENCE PERSONALLY
95% OF WHAT WE TEACH TO OTHERS.

— WILLIAM GLASSER

15 WAYS TO SAVE IN COLLEGE

1 Buy books online or rent books.

2 Get the 14 meal plan instead of the 21 meal plan.

3 Shop at local grocery stores instead of the campus food markets....and don't go to the grocery store when you are hungry.

4 Attend campus activities and events that have free food.

5 Share Uber and Lyft rides.

6 Instead of going to expensive off-campus places on the weekends, look for free activities on campus and google free activities around the town.

7 If you have an article of clothing or an object you don't want and that is in good condition, try to sell it online.

8 If you are a science or math major, offer to tutor middle or high school students for a fee.

9 Resist the temptation to get a pet while you are in college—pets are expensive!!

10 Limit trips to coffee shop— they are expensive. Buy an inexpensive coffee pot and make your own coffee.

11 Think about becoming a residential advisor—most colleges and universities give free room and board.

12 Keep looking for grants, scholarships, awards and other financial options.

13 Keep low maintenance hair styles.....check out cosmetology schools in the area.

14 No online shopping.

15 Don't bring your credit card or debit card everywhere you go.

LIVE LIKE A COLLEGE STUDENT. YOU ARE NOT AN EXECUTIVE *YET*!

Friendship
ISN'T A BIG THING, IT'S A *million* SMALL THINGS.

— **UNKNOWN**

BEING HAPPY socially

Hang out with SMART people.

Give people a 2nd chance, but not a 3rd.

Be strong enough to stand up to PEER PRESSURE. Think about the consequences before you are tempted to do something risky or dangerous.

Make sure your apologies are meaningful. Don't be afraid to say you were wrong, you feel bad for what happened and ask how you can make it better.

Don't hang around with people who have personality traits you do not want to have.

Become a club president or form a new club.

Show RESPECT and behave well in the class even if you are the only one.

Be careful to whom you loan things to.

When you talk to people look them right in the eye.

WRITE THANK YOU NOTES!

Consider the **PROS & CONS** of Greek Life.

Don't assume your roommate will become your best friend.

Learn to write coherently clearly to convey ideas. This will set you apart when applying for a position after college.

The best time to make friends is before you need them.

Be responsible and sensible at parties. Stay **SAFE** and know how to avoid problems.

KNOW YOUR LIMITS.

It's OK to be a **NERD.** They usually become the big winners in their careers.

Show *RESPECT* for secretaries, custodians, cafeteria workers, and anyone else who "works" for a living.

If your living arrangement is not satisfactory, start making plans to move.

If you need to work consider a meaningful job like working at the IT desk or assisting a professor. A job on campus rather than an off campus job will save a lot of time.

When you lose a friend by lending him some money, you get the best of the bargain.

Think of your dorm as a place to socialize & sleep and not to study. Make it a point to try to go 5 nights a week after dinner to the library or study area. If you do this consistently, you should complete your studying by 8:30- 9:00pm.

Attend the many college sponsored events like lectures given by important people, sporting competitions, concerts, plays, and movies---you already paid for them!

Stay in touch with your college friends over the summer.

Learn to say **"NO"** to people and activities that may keep you from achieving your goals. Look out for #1 (yourself)

Be interested in students from other countries and those from different 7 backgrounds. You can learn a lot about their customs and cultures.

Develop your social skills as well as your academic skills.

You will be meeting a lot of people all the time. Don't forget that first impressions are important.

A great place to meet people is at the swimming pool and recreation center.

BE YOURSELF.
EVERYONE ELSE IS TAKEN.

—

OSCAR WILDE

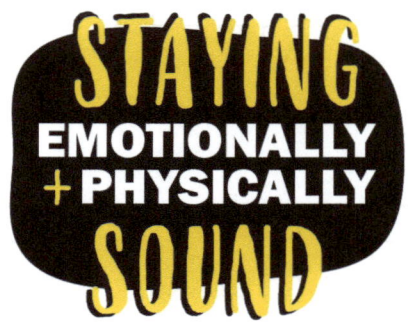

Staying Emotionally + Physically Sound

+ Accept that there are always going to be people who can do things better than you.

+ As soon as you recognize symptoms of becoming ill, start remedies. This may mean forgoing a party to sleep or visiting the health center before your illness gets worse.

SPEND SOME TIME ALONE EVERY DAY.

GET ENOUGH SLEEP! A TIRED MIND IS A CLOSED MIND.

+ Take responsibility for your own learning. Don't blame others for your poor grades.

+ Sometimes volunteering can provide lots of satisfaction by helping others in the community.

+ Friendships can start anywhere—in the classroom, cafeteria, at the gym, sporting events, and wherever people gather.

+ Don't be afraid to say, "I don't know" or "I need help".

+ Take lots of pictures because you'll be glad you did this 20 years from now.

+ You may have been the center of your parent's universe but those days are over. You're not going to be the center of anyone's universe in college.

+ If the level of work is beyond your ability, you may not be prepared to meet the academic demands.

+ Consider a remedial course or resources at the academic college support center.

> **EXPECT YOUR INTERESTS AND PREFERENCES TO CHANGE.**

+ Stay open-minded. You can't learn with a closed mind.

> **FAILURE IS A PART OF LIFE LEARN TO DEAL WITH IT.**

+ A lot of your education will be learned outside of class.

+ Don't let the Freshman 15 become the Freshman 20!

+ Not everything will work out as planned. Accept it, get over it, and move on.

+ Anxiety issues are most likely the result of poor grades, not the cause of poor grades.

+ Don't lose touch with your high school friends, family, and relatives. They are the ones who nurtured you to become the person you are.

+ Understand that success in college is more than your GPA and your degree. It's also about integrity, honesty, generosity, confidence, empathy, politeness, and respect. These traits do not happen by chance.

> **WHEN YOU HIRE SOMEONE SMARTER THAN YOU, YOU PROVE THAT YOU ARE SMARTER THAN THEY ARE.**

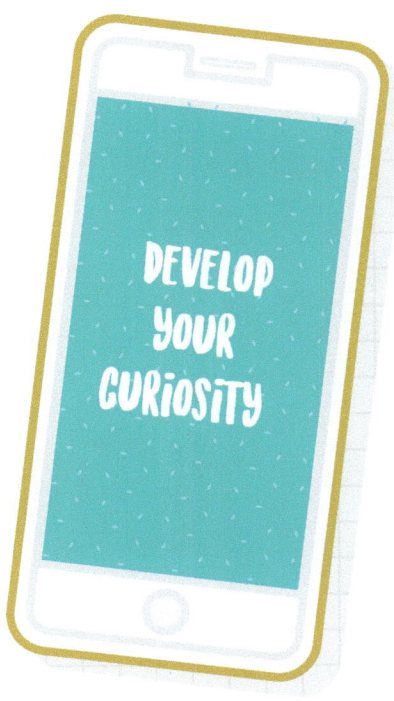

DEVELOP YOUR CURIOSITY

NO ONE CAN MAKE YOU FEEL INFERIOR WITHOUT YOUR CONSENT.

ELEANOR ROOSEVELT

Planning AHEAD

1
VISIT THE CAREER CENTER...

and take an interest inventory, vocational/ career inventory, learn about internships, and start writing a resume. Find out the types of jobs related to your major. During your freshman year, the career center will help you get started on writing your resume.

2
START A PORTFOLIO

Start collecting all the returned papers, projects, tests, comments from professors that will make you feel proud. Remember, it's what you do outside of class that is almost as important as what you do in class.

3
LEARN TO WRITE WELL.

Although you may be a good writer, you will become a better writer if you go to the writing center. Skilled writers are hard to find because it's rare to become a skilled writer without instruction.

4
BE THE ONE WHO'S ALWAYS ON TIME

5
RECOGNIZE ADMIRABLE TRAITS

and talents of friends and others that you might want to acquire.

6
LEARN TO RESIST TEMPTATION

7
TAKE PLENTY OF PICTURES

8
PLAN TO TAKE

a few courses outside your major.

9
START BUILDING A RESUME

10
DON'T WAIT UNTIL..
the day before to write a 15 page paper that was assigned a month ago.

TO LEARN

IF PLAN A FAILS, REMEMBER THERE ARE 25 OTHER LETTERS.

CHRIS GUILLEBEAU

STAYING ON TRACK TO GRADUATE

- TRY NOT TO STRETCH FOUR YEARS INTO FIVE.

- Being smart is great but a solid work ethic is even greater.

- Consider taking an online course the semester before you take your most challenging course if you feel you lack background knowledge.

- KEEP YOUR WORK AREA CLEAN AND CLEAR OF CLUTTER

- KEEP AN UPDATED RESUME

- GO TO EVERY CAREER FAIR AND TRY TO FIND A SUMMER INTERNSHIP

- Internships increase hiring power. They set you apart and let you sample various occupations.

- Research shows that students who email, text, and listen to music during class learn, remember, and understand less and receive lower grades as compared to those who give undivided attention.

- Taking 12 credits a semester is considered full time but if you want to graduate in four years, you will have to average 15 credits a semester.

- MAKE AN APPOINTMENT AT THE CAREER COUNSELING CENTER TO TAKE ADVANTAGE OF ALL THEY OFFER

YOUR TICKET TO THE UPPER MIDDLE CLASS IS A COLLEGE DEGREE

A FAILING OR BAD GRADE IS NOT THE END OF THE WORLD

This suggestion is for the serious students. When beginning to learn something new, try to really delve into it. Get a few books on the subject, use internet resources, and try to become knowledgeable in that area.

Check in with your advisors often to make sure you are on track for graduation.

Your college may not be considered an "elite" school. That's OK, because the name of your college doesn't mean as much as all the activities, awards, internships, and opportunities you can put on a resume.

ASKING FOR HELP IS OK AND OFTEN THE MOST IMPORTANT STEP TOWARD PROGRESS

If you have a job while attending college, remember that college must come first, no matter how much money you are making from a part-time job.

> I'VE MISSED MORE THAN 9000 SHOTS IN MY CAREER. I'VE LOST ALMOST 300 GAMES. TWENTY-SIX TIMES I'VE BEEN TRUSTED TO TAKE THE GAME WINNING SHOT AND MISSED. I'VE FAILED OVER AND OVER AND OVER AGAIN IN MY LIFE. AND THAT IS WHY I SUCCEED.

MICHAEL JORDAN

VOCABULARY

Most of the time a person's academic level can be determined by the words used in speaking and writing.

50 COMMON WORD PARTS

The 50 word parts listed on page 72 are used in hundreds and hundreds of words you will be coming across in college. We advise you to memorize them and their meaning.

THE BIG 205

We have compiled this list of 205 words that our freshman college students should know for their classes.

Check out the Big 205 list on page 73.

ALWAYS KEEP IN MIND THAT PEOPLE WILL JUDGE YOU BY THE WORDS

DID YOU KNOW?
THERE ARE 250 ROOTS, PREFIXES, & SUFFIXES THAT CAN BE COMBINED TO FORM OVER **1,000 WORDS?**

COLORS FADE, TEMPLES CRUMBLE, EMPIRES FALL BUT WORDS ENDURE.

EDWARD THORNDIKE

THE AVERAGE HIGH SCHOOL GRADUATE KNOWS: **15,000 WORDS**

FOUR YEARS LATER MOST GRADUATES KNOW: **30,000 WORDS**

50 COMMON WORD PARTS

a
aero, ante, anti, auto

m
mal, micro, migr, mis

b
bene, bi, bio

o
omni

r
rupt

c
cent, cogn, cycl

p
pac, para, patri, peri, phil, phobia, phon, post, pre, pseudo

d
dec, demo, dia, dis

e
ex

f
fin

s
spec, sub, sym

g
graph, greg

l
lay

t
terra, thermos

h
hyper, hypo, hydro

u
uni

v
vert

THE BIG 205

-A-
abridge
abyss
acrid
advocate
aesthetic
aghast
advocate
agnostic
allusion
ambiguity
ambivalence
amenable
analogy
apathy
assumption
astute
autonomy

-B-
bandanna
benevolence
bequeath
biofeedback
boon
bucolic

-C-
candor
cantankerous
capricious
charlatan
chastise
clandestine
cliche'
cognition
colloquial
concur
condone
connive
connotation
consensus
contempt
convene
culpable

-D-
decimate
deductive
definitive
delude
denotation
deprecate
description
diaphanous
dichotomy
discord
description
disinclined
divulge
dour
duplicity
duress

-E-
elicit
elucidate
elude
empathy
eminent
emporium
enervate
entrée
epicure
epitaph
epitome
erudite
ethics
ethos
etymology
euphemism
exposition

-F-
fallacy
fastidious
feasible
flaccid
flaunt
flout
fortuitous
frivolous

-G-
gargantuan
generation
genteel
gratuitous
gregarious
grievous
gullible
guttural

-H-
haphazard
herculean
hieroglyphics
homage
horde
hover

-I-
idiom
illicit
imperil
implore
imply
inane
incorrigible
inculcate
inductive
infer
inhibition
innuendo
insidious
intrepid
introvert
irony

-J-
jargon
jocularity
judicious
juxtaposition

-L-
latent
longevity
logos

-M-
maladaptive
malefactor
maudlin
maxim
meander
melancholy
memoirs
mercurial
metropolis
mimicry
minutiae
mitigate

-N-
narcissism
neophyte
nonchalant
noxious

-O-
objective
omnipotent
omniscient
ostracism

-P-
panacea
paradox
paragon
pathos
pejorative
penury
perennial
perfunctory

peripatetic
perseverance
peruse
placebos
plagiarism
posthumous
potpourri
preposterous
presumptuous
proclivity
prodigious
profligate
prognosis
prudent

-Q-
quintessence
quixotic

-R-
recalcitrant
redundancy
remorseful
reproach
resilient
revenge
revoke
rhetoric

-S-
sarcasm
sardonic
scapegoat
secular
segregate
somatic
sporadic

stereotype
subjective
subjugate
succinct
suppression
sycophant

-T-

taboos
taciturn
theory
tirade
topography
tortuous
transient
tryst

-V-

validity
vicarious
visage

-W-

wit

FOREIGN WORDS
too good to miss!

à la carte
French

alma mater
Latin

carte blanche
French

caveat emptor
Latin

cul de sac
French

faux pas
French

ombudsman
Swedish

status quo
Latin

verbatim
Latin

Final THOUGHTS

You have "Taken the Challenge" and are now a better prepared college student.

We hope you have enjoyed all of our "tips" and recommendations and will use many of them. Remember, that the time in college will be like no other time in your life---and it will go by very quickly.

We hope you are the kind of student who not only earns a degree but also has a lot of fantastic, enriching experiences.

We urge you to keep this book and reread it before every semester begins!

Kay Lopate and Patsy Self Trand

P.S. Don't forget to fill out the letter to yourself on the following pages during graduation week!!

On the next page, write a letter to yourself.

On the next page, write another letter to yourself during the week of your graduation. Again, each paragraph begins with a sentence starter. All you need to do is to add 2-3 sentences to complete the paragraph. You will be glad you did this and you will treasure these memories years from now.

Again, our congratulations to you!!!

Graduation date: _____

Dear: _____

As I prepare to walk across the stage I feel:
_____
_____ about graduation.

I also feel: _____
_____

I'm a little nervous about: _____
_____

All in all, the college experience has been:
_____
_____

To celebrate graduation, we plan to: _____
_____
_____

I have invited the following people to attend the graduation ceremony: _____
_____
_____

After graduation, I plan to: _____
The advice I would give an incoming freshman is:
_____
_____

Regards to myself,

_____

About the AUTHORS

Kay Lopate is a Professor Emeritus from the University of Miami, Miami, FL where she co-founded the Reading and Study Skills Center and taught for College of Education. Her special interests are preparing PreMed students for medical school and helping undergraduate students acquire advanced reading abilities to succeed in the demands of mastering college level textbooks.

Patsy Self Trand is a faculty member of Florida International University and former administrator of the Reading and Learning Lab. Dr. Trand teaches undergraduate, honors, and graduate courses for the FIU School of Arts and Sciences. She is committed to pass her wealth of knowledge and experience to help high school and college students reach their academic goals. She has authored many articles and has presented at many national and international conferences.

www.ingramcontent.com/pod-product-compliance
Lightning Source LLC
Chambersburg PA
CBHW042331150426
43194CB00001B/18